First Time

Getting a Haircut

Melinda Radabaugh

Heinemann Library
Chicago, Illinois

Designed by Sue Emerson, Heinemann Library
Printed and bound in the United States by Lake Book Manufacturing, Inc.

07 06 05 04 03
10 9 8 7 6 5 4 3 2 1

Library of Congress Cataloging-in-Publication Data
Radabaugh, Melinda Beth.
    Getting a haircut / Melinda Beth Radabaugh.
        p. cm. -- (First time)
Summary: Describes what to expect on your first visit to the barber shop or salon for a haircut, discussing the big chairs, smocks, shampoo, haircutting tools, and blow-dryer.
    ISBN 1-4034-0225-6 (HC), 1-4034-0464-X (Pbk.)
    1. Haircutting--Juvenile literature. [1. Haircutting.] I. Title. II. Series.
TT970 .R33 2002
646.7'24--dc21

2002000934

Acknowledgments
The author and publishers are grateful to the following for permission to reproduce copyright material:
p. 4 Norbert Schafer/Corbis; p. 5L George Shelley/Corbis; p. 5R Bob Krist/Corbis; p. 6 Charles Gupton/Corbis; p. 7L Robert Lifson/Heinemann Library; p. 7R Eyewire Collection/Getty Images; pp. 8, 9, 12, 13, 16, 18, 19T, 20, 21, 24T Greg Williams/Heinemann Library; p. 10 Linda Phillips/PhotoResearchers; p. 11 Evan Kafka/Liaison/Getty Images; p. 14 Jack Ballard/Visuals Unlimited; p. 15 Summer Productions; p. 17 Amor Montes De Oca; p. 19B Roger Ressmeyer/Corbis; p. 22 (row 1, L–R) Greg Williams/Heinemann Library, PhotoDisc; p. 22 (row 2, L–R) John A. Rizzo/Getty Images, PhotoDisc; p. 22 (row 3, L–R) Greg Williams/Heinemann Library, RDF/Visuals Unlimited; p. 23 (row 1) Greg Williams/Heinemann Library; p. 23 (row 2, L–R) Eyewire Collection/Getty Images, Greg Williams/Heinemann Library, Greg Williams/Heinemann Library; p. 23 (row 3, L–R) PhotoDisc, Bob Krist/Corbis, Jack Ballard/Visuals Unlimited; p. 24 (top, L–R) Greg Williams/Heinemann Library, PhotoDisc; p. 24B PhotoDisc; back cover (L–R) PhotoDisc, Greg Williams/Heinemann Library

Cover photograph by Greg Williams/Heinemann Library
Photo research by Amor Montes de Oca

Every effort has been made to contact copyright holders of any material reproduced in this book. Any omissions will be rectified in subsequent printings if notice is given to the publisher.

Special thanks to our advisory panel for their help in the preparation of this book:

Eileen Day, Preschool Teacher
Chicago, IL

Ellen Dolmetsch,
Library Media Specialist
Wilmington, DE

Kathleen Gilbert,
Second Grade Teacher
Round Rock, TX

Sandra Gilbert,
Library Media Specialist
Houston, TX

Angela Leeper,
Educational Consultant
North Carolina Department
of Public Instruction
Raleigh, NC

Pam McDonald,
Reading Support Specialist
Winter Springs, FL

Melinda Murphy,
Library Media Specialist
Houston, TX

Special thanks to the Vance and Opp families for their assistance with the photographs in this book.

Some words are shown in bold, **like this.**
You can find them in the picture glossary on page 23.

Contents

Why Do You Need a Haircut?

Some people like short hair.

They cut it when it looks long.

Some people want a new **hairstyle.**

A haircut is a different hairstyle.

Where Do You Get a Haircut?

Some children get a haircut at home.

A grown-up cuts their hair.

Some children go to a **salon**.

Other children go to a **barbershop**.

What Is a Barbershop?

A **barbershop** is a place to get a haircut.

Inside there are chairs and big mirrors.

A **barber** cuts people's hair.

What Is a Salon?

A **salon** is a place to get a
new **hairstyle.**

You can get a haircut there, too.

Inside, there are chairs and big mirrors.

A **stylist** cuts people's hair.

What Happens at a Barbershop?

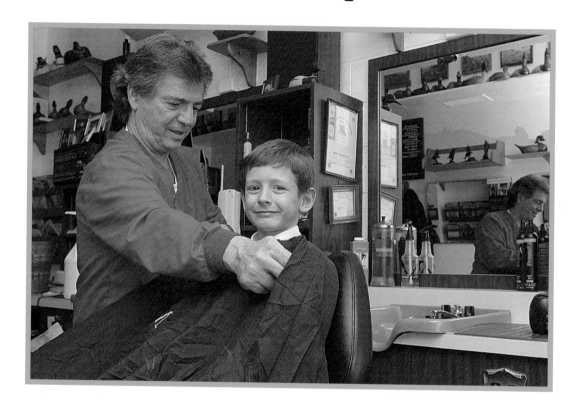

You sit in a big chair.

The **barber** puts a **cape** on you.

The cape keeps hair off your clothes.

The barber combs your hair.

What Happens at a Salon?

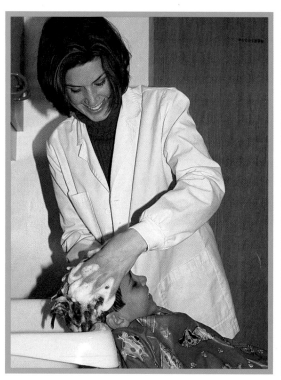 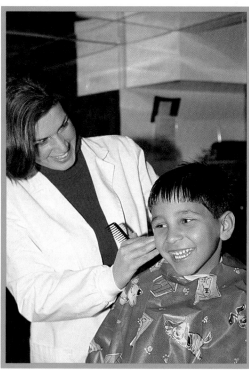

The **stylist** might wash your hair.

Then, you sit in the stylist's chair.

The stylist cuts your hair.

Then she dries it with a **blow-dryer**.

What Will They Use to Cut Your Hair?

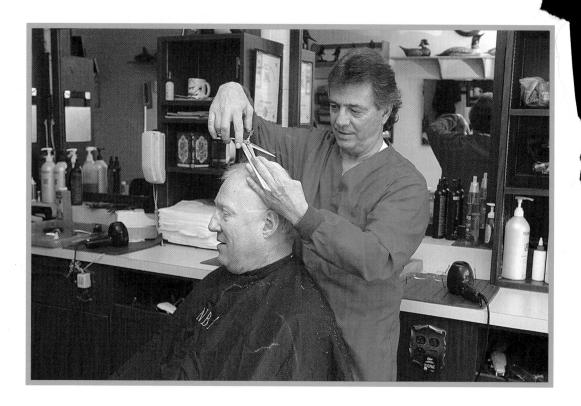

Barbers and stylists cut hair with shears.

Sometimes they use **clippers**.

How Does a Haircut Feel?

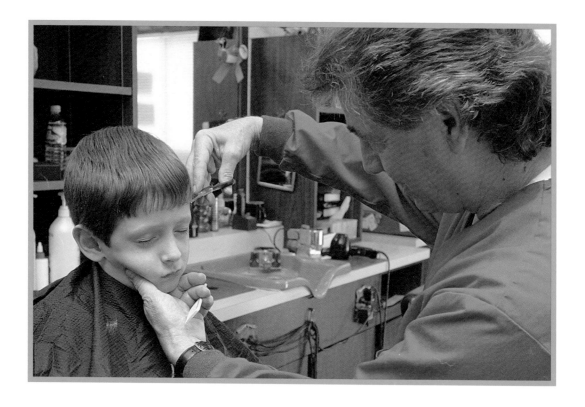

A haircut does not hurt.

But you need to sit very still.

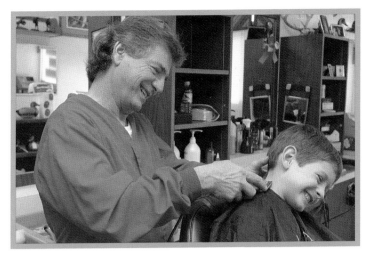

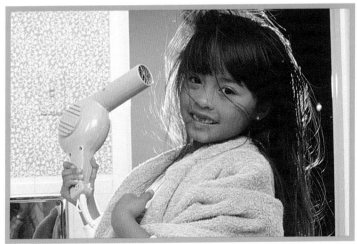

Clippers buzz and tickle.

The air from a **blow-dryer** feels warm.

What Happens Next?

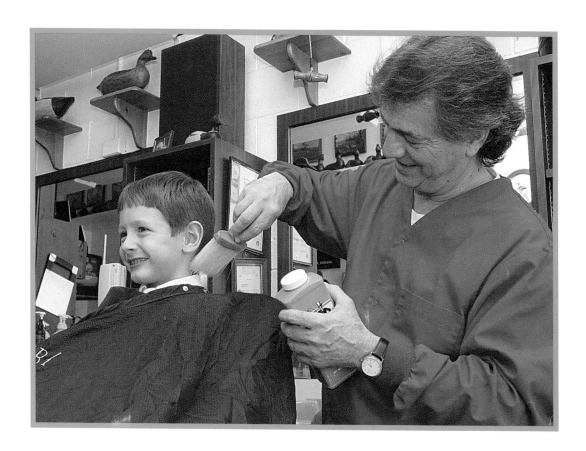

The **barber** or **stylist** will brush off little hairs.

Off comes the **cape!**

You can see your haircut in the mirror.

You pay for your haircut and go home.

Quiz

What will you find at the **barbershop** or **salon?**

Look for the answers on page 24.

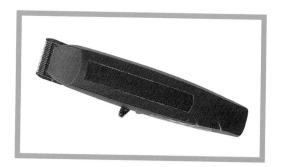

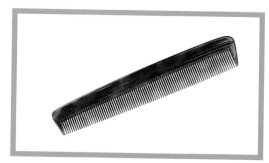

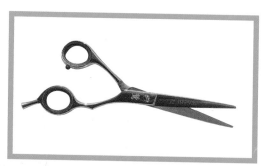

Picture Glossary

barber
pages 9, 12, 13, 16, 20

cape
pages 12, 13, 20

salon
pages 7, 10–11, 14, 22

barbershop
pages 7, 8–9, 12, 22

clippers
pages 17, 19

shears
page 16

blow-dryer
pages 15, 19

hairstyle
pages 5, 10

stylist
pages 11, 14, 15, 16, 20

Note to Parents and Teachers

Reading for information is an important part of a child's literacy development. Learning begins with a question about something. Help children think of themselves as investigators and researchers by encouraging their questions about the world around them. Each chapter in this book begins with a question. Read the question together. Look at the pictures. Talk about what you think the answer might be. Then read the text to find out if your predictions were correct. Think of other questions you could ask about the topic, and discuss where you might find the answers. Assist children in using the picture glossary and the index to practice new vocabulary and research skills.

Index

Answers to quiz on page 22

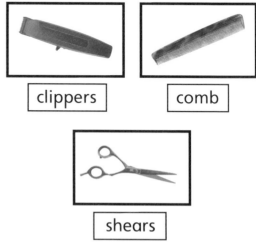

clippers

comb

shears